INTERFACT

THE BOOK AND DISK THAT W

™

G000054476

EGYPTIANS

™

PRINCETON ■ LONDON

Book and disk by
act-two Ltd

Published in the United States and Canada by
Two-Can Publishing LLC
234 Nassau Street
Princeton, NJ 08542

This edition Copyright © 2000 Two-Can Publishing LLC

For information on other Two-Can books and multimedia,
Call 1-609-921-6700, fax 1-609-921-3349, or visit our web site at
http://www.two-canpublishing.com

ISBN: 1-58728-458-8

2 4 6 8 10 9 7 5 3 1

Photographic Credits: Front cover Superstock
p.9, p.21 (left), p.23 (bottom), p.25 (bottom), p.26, p.28 (right), p.34 (left) Werner Forman Archives;
p.10 Sonia Halliday; p.10, p.14, p.15 (right), p.16, p.17, p.19, p.20, p.23 (top), p.25(top), p.27, p.28 (left),
p.34 (right) Micheal Holford; p.15 (left), p.21 (right), p.24, p.25 (centre) Ronald Sheridan.
All illustrations by Jon Davis of Linden Artists except those on page 29–33, which are Maxine Hamil.

Printed in Hong Kong by Wing King Tong

INTERFACT

INTERFACT will have you hooked in minutes — and that's a fact!

● **The disk is full of interactive activities, puzzles, quizzes, and games that are fun to do and packed with interesting facts.**

The Sphinx has the answers to all your questions.

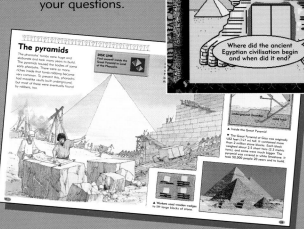

The pyramids

The pharaohs' tombs were huge and elaborate and took many years to build. The pyramids housed the bodies of some early pharaohs. There was so much riches inside that tomb-robbing became very common. To prevent this, pharaohs had mastaba vaults built underground, but most of these were eventually found by robbers, too.

DISK LINK
Find yourself inside the Great Pyramid in Land of the Pharaohs.

▲ Inside the Great Pyramid

► The Great Pyramid at Giza was originally 482 feet (147 m) tall. It contained more than 2 million stone blocks. Each block weighed about 2.5 short tons (2.3 metric tons), and some were much bigger. The pyramid was covered in white limestone. It took 50,000 people 20 years to build.

▲ Workers used wooden wedges to lift large blocks of stone.

Where did the ancient Egyptian civilisation begin and when did it end?

Click on Ramses to ask a question

● **Open the book and discover more fascinating information, highlighted with lots of full-color illustrations and photographs.**

How did the Egyptians manage to build such huge pyramids? Read up and find out.

● To get the most out of **INTERFACT,** use the book and disk together. Look out for the special signs called Disk Links and Bookmarks. To find out more, turn to page 43.

23

BOOKMARK

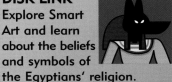

DISK LINK
Explore Smart Art and learn about the beliefs and symbols of the Egyptians' religion.

Once you've launched **INTERFACT,** you'll never look back.

LOAD UP!
Go to **page 40** to find out how to load your disks and click into action.

3

What's on the disk

HELP SCREEN

Learn how to use the disk in no time at all.

These are the controls the Help Screen will tell you how to use:
- arrow keys
- reading boxes
- "hot" words

LAND OF THE PHARAOHS

An interactive adventure story in which you are the hero!

This is a story about ancient Egypt, but what happens in it is up to you! Use the things you've learned about Egypt to foil the plotters' plan, save the pharaoh, and bring about a happy ending.

RIDDLE OF THE SPHINX

If you've got a question, the Sphinx has the answer!

Click on Ramses the Camel to ask all sorts of questions about the ancient Egyptians. Then click on the Sphinx to hear the answers!

SMART ART

Take a closer look at an ancient Egyptian wall painting.

Examine a real Egyptian painting on screen and discover what's going on. Find out what the Egyptians believed would happen to them when they died.

I WANT MY MUMMY

A guide to mummy making – Egyptian style!

Then, the embalmer stuck his hand right inside and pulled out all the internal organs. He removed everything except the heart.

What's the secret to making a marvelous mummy? Find out everything you ever wanted to know about mummification with this step-by-step guide!

JOURNEY OF DISCOVERY

Set off on a journey of discovery down the river Nile.

Test your knowledge of ancient Egypt as you try to sail from the temple of ancient Abu Simbel to the Great Pyramid of Giza. You'll need to think fast if you want to stay afloat!

WRITE AWAY

Create your own messages using Egyptian hieroglyphs.

Learn all about ancient Egyptian writing. Then type in your own message and turn it into a secret hieroglyphic code!

SENET

How to play the pharaohs' favorite game!

Learn how to play the most popular board game in ancient Egypt. Then challenge a friend to a match. Your computer will explain all the rules!

What's in the book

8 **The Egyptian world**
How Egypt became a
powerful civilization

10 **The gift of the Nile**
All about the river Nile –
why is it so precious?

12 **The pharaoh**
Learn all about the
pharaohs and their power

14 **Gods and temples**
Who did the ancient
Egyptians worship?

16 **The afterlife**
What the Egyptians believed
about life after death

18 **The pyramids**
All about how the famous
pyramids were built

20 **Writing and education**
Did ancient Egyptian
children go to school?

22 **At home**
All about the design of
ancient Egyptian houses

24 **Work and play**
How did Egyptians enjoy
their leisure time?

26 **Food**
The Egyptians' diet and
the crops they grew

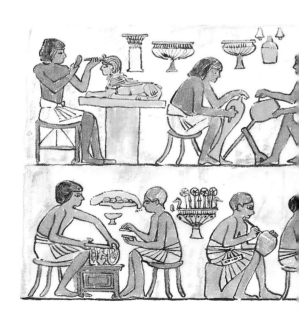

*All words in the text that appear in **bold** can be found in the glossary*

28 **Clothes**
What were the ancient Egyptian fashions?

29 **Nut's children**
A story about why the moon changes shape

34 **How we know**
Important evidence revealed

35 **Glossary**
Key words defined

36 **Lab pages**
Note pages you can photocopy and use

38 **Rules of senet**
How to play the Egyptian game on your disk

40 **Loading your INTERFACT disk**
How to load your disk

42 **How to use INTERFACT**
Easy-to-follow instructions

44 **Troubleshooting**
Got a problem? Find the solution here!

46 **Index**
The quick route to information

LOWER EGYPT

GIZA ● ● **MEMPHIS**

Giza is the site of the Great **Pyramid**.

Memphis was the first capital of the united Egypt.

UPPER EGYPT

VALLEY OF THE KINGS ●

● **THEBES**

First Cataract

Thebes was the religious capital of the New Kingdom.

Many pharaohs were buried in the Valley of the Kings in tombs cut out of rock.

ABU SIMBEL ●

The temple of Abu Simbel

Second Cataract

Third Cataract

Fourth Cataract

RED SEA

Cataracts are places on the Nile where the river flows through dangerous rapids and waterfalls.

Blue Nile

White Nile

The Egyptian world

The Egyptian **civilization** began more than 5,000 years ago, when Menes, the ruler of Upper Egypt, conquered Lower Egypt and united both kingdoms. The Egyptians never forgot that Egypt had been two lands, and the **pharaoh** was known as the "king of Upper and Lower Egypt."

For the next 2,000 years, Egypt remained powerful and expanded to take over new lands. The Egyptians were sophisticated people who developed architecture and new, efficient methods of government and made important discoveries in medicine and astronomy.

▼ The Great Sphinx, a statue with the head of a man and the body of a lion, stands in the desert near the pyramids of Giza. Scholars believe the huge statue was built for Khafre, a pharaoh who lived about 4,500 years ago.

DISK LINK
Why was Egypt such a powerful nation? Find out in Riddle of the Sphinx.

The gift of the Nile

Ancient Egypt was a long, narrow country running along the length of the Nile River, an oasis surrounded by desert. A Greek writer named Herodotus arrived in Egypt and called the country the "gift of the Nile" because it was the Nile that provided most of Egypt's wealth. The rest of Egypt was barren and rocky, with little water. This desert, which the ancient Egyptians called the Red Land, could not support much life, though the Egyptians found precious stones and metals there.

Once a year the **Akhet,** or **Inundation,** came, flooding the river valley from July to September. When the water withdrew, it left behind rich, fertile black mud – called the Black Land. The amount of floodwater was very important. Too little meant that the crops would fail and there would be famine, too much and the water could sweep away people, livestock, and houses.

For this reason, the Nile's water level was constantly measured with a device known as a **nilometer**, and the changing seasons were carefully monitored to try to prevent famine. To identify the changing seasons, the Egyptians studied the cycle of the sun, the moon, and the stars. The results of their studies led them to divide the year into 365 days, grouped into 12 months, each containing 30 days – with five days left over.

◄ The Egyptians also depended on the Nile for transportation. Heavy loads were dragged to and from river barges on rollers or sledges. They usually did not use carts with wheels because they were useless in the desert sands and in the mud.

DISK LINK
Would you like to take a trip down the Nile? You can – it certainly will be a Journey of Discovery!

▼ The green and fertile land around the Nile stands out against the barren desert that surrounds it.

The pharaoh

The pharaoh was an **absolute ruler**, answerable to no one. His word was law. Another way to say "justice" was "what the pharaoh loves," and "wrongdoing" was "what the pharaoh hates."

The pharaoh was seen as a god. He married his own sister or half-sister so that his children would have the blood of gods. He often had many other wives, too. His subjects treated him with all the reverence they gave to their other gods, kneeling before him with their foreheads touching the ground. As a sign of respect, they never referred to him by his own name, but used official names instead. One of these was *per-ao,* meaning great house, which is where the word *pharaoh* comes from.

A system was set up to govern the empire's 5 million people. The pharaoh's chief adviser, or **vizier**, was the second most powerful person. Many governors called **nomarchs** served under the vizier's rule. Each nomarch was in charge of a region, or nome. They ensured that everyone paid taxes. Payments were in the form of goods or services because the Egyptians did not use money.

▼ The pharaoh had many public obligations.

DISK LINK
You can take part in a thrilling adventure story when you find yourself in the Land of the Pharaohs.

Famous pharaohs

About 300 pharaohs reigned during Egypt's long history. Some were great warriors or governors. But many have been forgotten, except for their names.

Tutankhamen
Tutankhamen was just a boy when he became pharaoh. During his ten-year reign, he restored order after the pharaoh Akhenaton had caused chaos by trying to introduce a new religion. Tutankhamen started building a number of temples to honor the god Amon-Re.

Thutmose III
Thutmose, the greatest warrior pharaoh, conquered Palestine and Syria and never lost a battle.

Cleopatra VII
Cleopatra was one of few women pharaohs. She formed an alliance with the Romans through **Julius Caesar** and then married **Mark Antony**. She killed herself after a military defeat.

Gods and temples

Religion was a very important part of Egyptian life. The Egyptians believed that gods took care of every event or problem. These gods often took the shape of a particular animal. Bast, the goddess of joy and love, usually was shown as a cat, and Anubis, the god who protected tombs, was shown as a jackal or as a man with a jackal's head.

Each god had a temple, where people could come to worship and ask favors. A statue of the god stood in a room in the temple. It was brought out only on feast days and even then it was hidden inside a shrine. People went only as far as the temple's entrance hall, where they would meet the priest. He would take messages and offerings and tell the people the god's answers. Animals often were kept in the temple.

The temple was considered to be the home of the god. Each day, meals were laid as offerings before his or her statue. Later, the food was removed and often eaten by the priests.

▼ The temple of Amon at Karnak was developed by many pharaohs until it was as big as six huge cathedrals.

DISK LINK
Find out more about the symbols and beliefs of the ancient Egyptian religion in Smart Art.

Important gods

RE was the sun-god. He took on different shapes at different times of the day. **AMON** was the god of the air and of Thebes. His name means hidden. He merged with Re to become the chief god, Amon-Re. **OSIRIS** was the god of the dead, who judged all people when they died. **ISIS** was the sister-wife of Osiris and the goddess and protector of women.

AMON

OSIRIS

ISIS

▶ This painting shows Hathor, goddess of music and love, as a cow.

▲ The jackal was sacred to Anubis.

15

The afterlife

The Egyptians believed that with proper preparation, a person could live after death. This preparation involved preserving the dead person's body and providing it with all the food, furniture, tools, and riches it would need in the afterlife. Even the poorest people were buried with scraps of food.

Journey to the afterlife

The dead had to make a long and hazardous journey before they could enjoy the afterlife. They had to pass a giant serpent and a crocodile, avoid being caught in nets and a furnace, and escape being drowned or beheaded.

When the dead person reached the underworld, the god Anubis measured his or her heart against the Feather of Truth. If it balanced, he would be greeted by Osiris, but if not, the person would be eaten by a monster that was part crocodile, part lion, and part hippopotamus.

▼ Osiris waits to greet the dead person whose heart is being weighed by Anubis. Thoth, god of wisdom, records what is happening. Can you see the dead person?

DISK LINK
Want to know how the Egyptians made mummies? Play I Want My Mummy and learn!

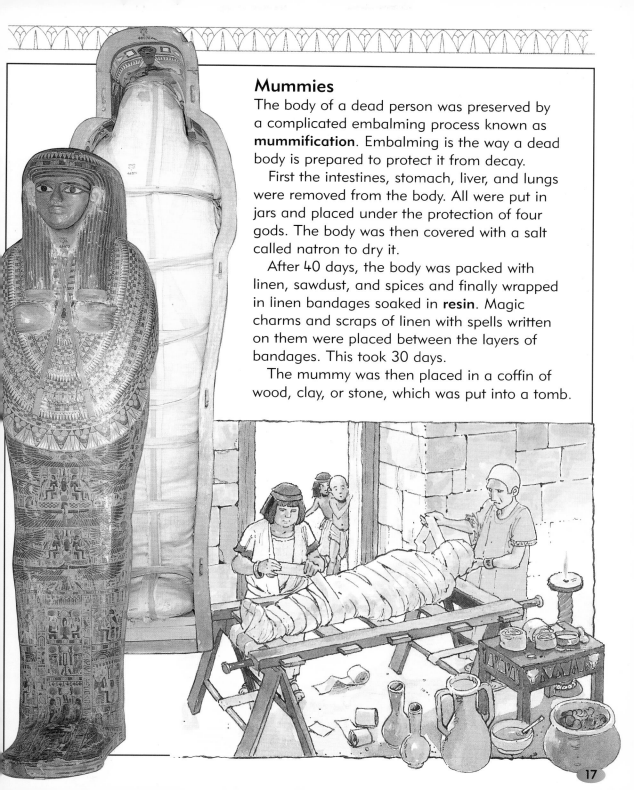

Mummies

The body of a dead person was preserved by a complicated embalming process known as **mummification**. Embalming is the way a dead body is prepared to protect it from decay.

First the intestines, stomach, liver, and lungs were removed from the body. All were put in jars and placed under the protection of four gods. The body was then covered with a salt called natron to dry it.

After 40 days, the body was packed with linen, sawdust, and spices and finally wrapped in linen bandages soaked in **resin**. Magic charms and scraps of linen with spells written on them were placed between the layers of bandages. This took 30 days.

The mummy was then placed in a coffin of wood, clay, or stone, which was put into a tomb.

The pyramids

The pharaohs' tombs were huge and elaborate and took many years to build. The pyramids housed the bodies of some early pharaohs. There were so many riches inside that tomb-robbing became very common. To prevent this, pharaohs had mazelike vaults built underground, but most of these were eventually found by robbers, too.

DISK LINK
Find yourself inside the Great Pyramid in Land of the Pharaohs.

▼ Workers built ramps of packed earth to move the stone blocks to the level where they were needed. Then the workers hauled the blocks up the ramp and put them into place by hand.

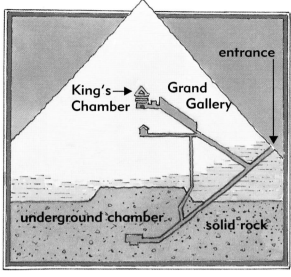

▲ Inside the Great Pyramid

▼ The Great Pyramid at Giza was originally 482 feet (147 m) tall. It contained more than 2 million stone blocks. Each block weighed about 2.5 short tons (2.3 metric tons), and some were much bigger. The pyramid was covered in white limestone. It took 50,000 people 20 years and to build.

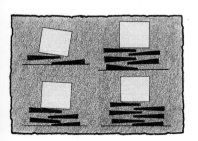

▲ Workers used wooden wedges to lift large blocks of stone.

Writing and education

Early Egyptians wrote using picture letters called **hieroglyphs**. There were more than 700 of these letters. Some stood for whole words. These were simple pictures for an object or action. For example, wavy lines meant water. Other symbols stood for one or two letters. There were no vowels in the alphabet, but the Egyptians managed without them. Try writing in English without vowels – would it be easy to read?

Hieroglyphs eventually became less detailed to make them quicker and easier to write. Scribes used these simpler symbols to create documents, such as tax records. Hieroglyphs were also used for writing on monuments and tombs.

The Egyptians used an early type of paper called **papyrus**, made from flattened, dried reed stems, stuck together to make pages. They wrote with thin, sharpened reeds dipped in ink.

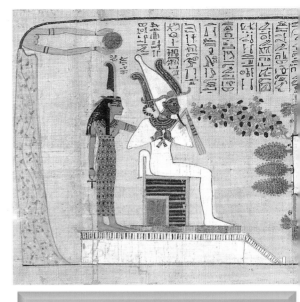

DISK LINK
Listen to the sounds of the hieroglyphs when you choose to play Write Away!

Learning

Most ancient Egyptians could not read or write. Many children were taught a trade by their parents. A few were trained to be scribes in schools and were taught math, astronomy, and writing. These schools were not very pleasant places to be. One scribe wrote, "The ears of a boy are in his back. He listens only when he is beaten."

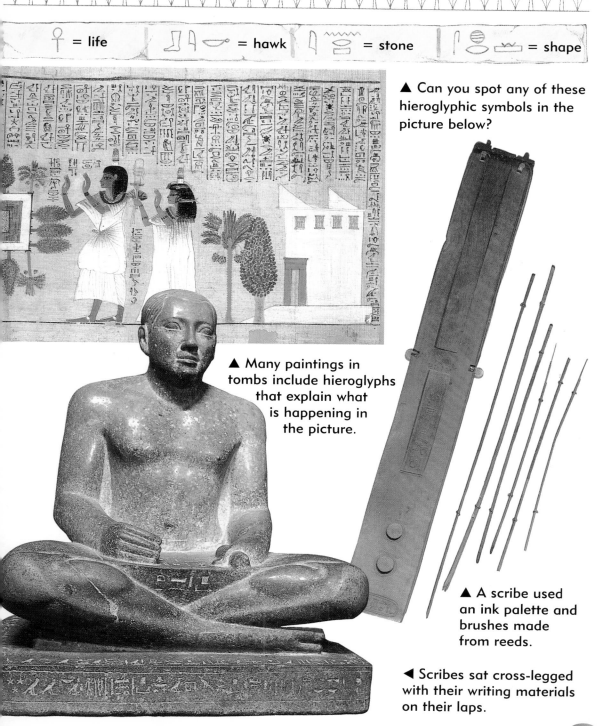

▲ Can you spot any of these hieroglyphic symbols in the picture below?

▲ Many paintings in tombs include hieroglyphs that explain what is happening in the picture.

▲ A scribe used an ink palette and brushes made from reeds.

◀ Scribes sat cross-legged with their writing materials on their laps.

At home

Egyptian houses were clustered together on the higher ground at the edge of the river's flood area. They were built of sunbaked brick made from mud and straw. In Egypt's hot, dry climate these bricks lasted a long time. Only buildings that were expected to last forever, like temples and tombs, were built of stone.

Houses were very plain, square buildings. They were often surrounded by a wall and had steps outside leading to a flat roof. Inside, the house was dark because of the tiny windows.

The man of the family used the front room of the house to conduct his trade. Sometimes, the family kept livestock in this room. Ordinary families had little furniture, just a chest for clothes and storage jars for food.

The second room was large, with small, high windows, and was used for receiving guests and eating meals. The kitchen, bathroom, and bedrooms were at the back of the house. Sometimes people cooked on the roof to avoid the risk of fire.

The houses of the rich looked like ordinary houses from the outside, but they were larger. They had wall paintings and paneling inside. These decorations could not be displayed outside because of the desert winds.

Furniture facts

● The Egyptians used little furniture. Most poor people usually had none and even the rich often sat on the floor.

● Much of the furniture was portable, like this folding wooden stool (right).

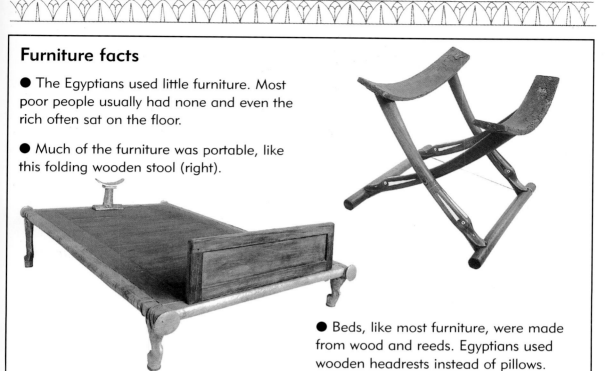

● Beds, like most furniture, were made from wood and reeds. Egyptians used wooden headrests instead of pillows.

Work and play

Work

Most Egyptians were farmers, but some had other jobs. A few were priests, scribes, and government officials. Many were craftworkers. Building the pyramids required hundreds of craftworkers: masons to carve the stone, draftsmen to design the structure, painters to decorate the walls, sculptors to carve statues, and other craftworkers to make the furniture, jewelry, and utensils that were put inside.

Because the Egyptians did not use money, the workers were paid with food, drink, clothes, and lodging. Sometimes, the workers building royal tombs went on strike if their payment did not arrive.

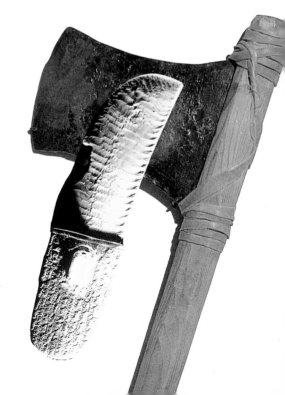

▶ Egyptian craftworkers used tools made from wood, bronze, and other metals.

Play

Egyptians worked very hard – sometimes for eight days in a row, followed by two days off. They spent their free time hunting, dancing, wrestling, playing games, and performing acrobatics. Rich people held lavish dinner parties, where guests were entertained by acrobats and musicians.

Board games also were popular, and **senet** was the favorite. It was played on a board divided into three rows of ten squares. Players tried to get all their pieces to the end of the board, while preventing the opponent from doing the same.

Children played with wooden balls as well as dolls and carved wooden animals.

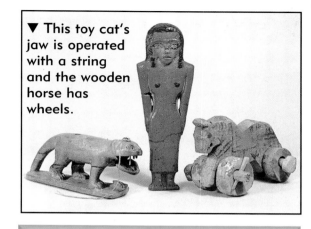

▼ This toy cat's jaw is operated with a string and the wooden horse has wheels.

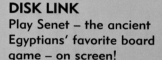

DISK LINK
Play Senet – the ancient Egyptians' favorite board game – on screen!

▶ This senet board has a little drawer to keep all the pieces in.

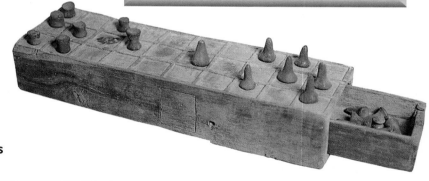

▼ Do you know what games these children are playing?

Food

The fertile soil around the Nile produced a variety of crops for the Egyptians. There was a large supply of wheat and barley for bread and beer. Egyptians also enjoyed onions, leeks, lettuce, and beans. They didn't have much fruit because it was hard to grow in the hot, dry climate, but they managed to grow figs, dates, grapes, and pomegranates.

People did not eat a great deal of meat. Cattle were used as working animals and for milk rather than meat. Feasts for the rich included a wide variety of meats, though, including strange delicacies such as antelope and hyena. For the most part, only the poor ate fish.

The Egyptians sat on the floor next to low tables and ate with their fingers. A servant washed the pharaoh's hands between each course.

Egyptian bread

Try making your own Egyptian bread. You can also add chopped dates.

You will need:
$3\frac{1}{4}$ cups (400 g) whole wheat flour
1 cup minus 2 tbsp (225 ml) water
$\frac{1}{2}$ tsp salt

Put the flour and salt in the bowl and add the water slowly, mixing well. Knead the dough and shape it into small rounds or triangles. Cover the shapes and let them sit overnight. Bake for 30 minutes at 350° F. (175° C).

● Mix the ingredients.

● Knead the dough.

● Cover the dough overnight before baking.

Farming facts

● There were three seasons in the farming year: the Inundation (June to October), the Emergence (November to January), when the floodwaters subsided, and the Drought (February to June).

● Each farmer's land was marked by heavy stones that could not be moved by the floods.

● A complex **irrigation** system allowed flood water to be stored in huge reservoirs so that it could be used when needed.

● During the Inundation, when little farm work could be done, many people worked on the pharaoh's building projects as a way of paying their taxes.

▼ Egyptian farmers used wooden plows pulled by oxen.

DISK LINK
Find out more about Egyptian farming methods in Riddle of the Sphinx.

Clothes

Most Egyptian people wore clothes made from linen. Flax, the plant from which linen is made, grows well in the Egyptian climate. Most people wore undyed linen. Only the rich could afford brightly colored cloth.

Men wore linen around their waists like a kilt or a simple tunic. Laborers wore linen loincloths or nothing at all. Men usually were clean-shaven or wore a small, pointed beard.

Women wore ankle-length dresses, with one or both shoulders bare. Most children wore nothing. Boys had shaved heads, except for a long plait on the right side of their head, which was called the lock of youth. In cold weather, everyone wore cloaks of wool or animal skins. Sandals were made from reeds or leather.

▲ Egyptian mirrors were made of bronze, and combs were made of ivory or wood.

Egyptian cosmetics

● The ancient Egyptians used highly perfumed oils to keep their skin healthy in the harsh desert winds.

● Rich Egyptian men and women wore wigs made from a mixture of real hair and vegetable fibers. The strands were attached to a netting base with wax.

● Men and women wore eye make-up to protect their eyes from sand and dust.

● At dinner parties, guests and servants wore wax cones of perfumed oil on their heads. The perfume gradually melted and ran down their hair and clothes.

Nut's children

The ancient Egyptians told many myths about their gods and about the world around them. Often these stories would try to explain an idea that many of the people did not understand. This story explains why the moon changes shape.

In long-ago times, Re, the chief of all the gods, still reigned on earth as a living pharaoh. He lived in a huge palace on the banks of the Nile, and all the people of Egypt came to bow down before him. All his courtiers did exactly what he asked, and he spent his time hunting, playing games, and feasting. It was a wonderful life!

However, one day a courtier came to him and told him about a conversation that he had overheard. Thoth, god of wisdom and magic, had told the goddess Nut that one day her son would be pharaoh of Egypt.

Re was furious. No one else was worthy of being pharaoh. He paced back and forth, shouting.

"How dare they suggest such a thing! No child of Nut will dethrone me!"

He thought for a long time. Eventually, summoning his magic powers, he said, "I lay this curse: No child of Nut will be born on any day or any night of any year."

News traveled quickly among the gods, so Nut soon heard of the curse. She was heartbroken. She wanted a child, but she knew that Re's magic was strong. How could she break the curse? The only god who might be able to help was Thoth, the wisest of all the gods, so she set off to see him at once.

Thoth loved Nut and, when he saw her tears, he decided to help her.

"I cannot lift Re's curse," he said, "but I may be able to get around it. Just wait."

Thoth knew that Khonsu, the moon-god, was a gambler, so he challenged him to a game of senet. Khonsu did not stop to think for a moment. He could not resist a challenge.

"Oh, Thoth," he said. "You may be the wisest god, but I am the greatest senet player ever. I have never lost a game. I will play you and I will win every game!"

The two sat down to play. From the start, Thoth won every game.

"You have been lucky, Thoth, that's all," said Khonsu. "I bet an hour of my light that I will win the next game."

But still he lost! Thoth kept on winning, and Khonsu kept on betting his own light until Thoth had won enough of Khonsu's light to equal five whole days.

Then Thoth stood up, thanked Khonsu, and left, taking Khonsu's light with him.

"What a coward," muttered Khonsu to himself. "My luck was just changing. I would have won the next game!"

Thoth fitted the five extra days in between the end of that year and the beginning of the next. At that time, a year was made up of twelve months, each with 30 days, making a total of 360 days in the year.

Nut was overjoyed when Thoth told her what he had done. Because the five extra days were not days in any year, Nut's children could be born on these days without breaking Re's curse.

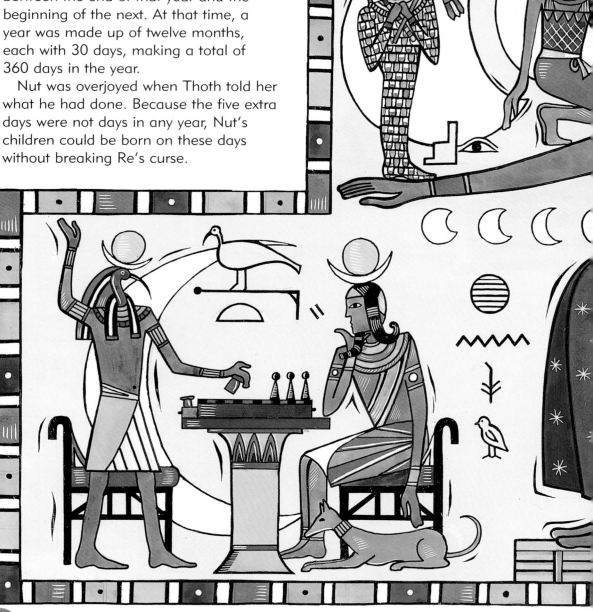

On the first day, Nut gave birth to Osiris, who was to be pharaoh after Re; on the second day to Harmachis, who is immortalized as the Sphinx; on the third day to Set, who later killed Osiris and became pharaoh; on the fourth day to Isis, who was to be the wife of Osiris, and on the fifth day to Nephthys, who was to be Set's wife.

As for Khonsu the moon-god, he was so weak after the game that he lost a lot of strength forever. He could no longer shine brightly all the time. Even today, the moon only shines brightly on a few days of the month and spends the rest of the time gathering its strength.

How we know

How do we know so much about the lives of the ancient Egyptians, even though they lived thousands of years ago?

Evidence from the ground

Archaeologists have pieced together a very clear picture of everyday Egyptian life both from the objects they have found in tombs and the paintings they have seen on tomb walls.

▲ Tomb paintings like this one give a detailed picture of life in ancient Egypt.

Evidence around us

Many people in Egypt today have a lifestyle similar to that of the ancient Egyptians. Farmers on the banks of the Nile live in houses that are built like the ancient houses, and certain farming methods are still the same. A huge dam built on the Nile now controls the flooding of the river and makes people's lives a great deal easier.

Evidence from books

The Egyptians were great writers. Scribes recorded everything in minute detail, and many of these records survive today. It is thanks to them that we know so much about the ancient Egyptians.

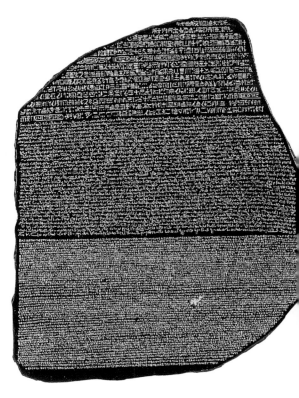

▲ It was not until 1822, some time after the **Rosetta Stone** had been discovered, that Egyptian texts could be read. The stone contains writing in hieroglyphs, in an Egyptian script called **demotic,** and in Greek. This and other tablets were used to translate hieroglyphs.

Glossary

An **absolute ruler** is someone who can make laws without consulting any other people.

The **Akhet** is the Egyptian word for the yearly flooding season on the Nile.

A **civilization** is an organized society that has well-developed customs, government, technology, and arts.

The **demotic** language is a form of ancient Egyptian writing that was developed beginning in 700 B.C. and was used for business and administration.

A **hieroglyph** is a symbol standing for a word or group of letters, used in Egyptian writing.

Inundation is a modern term that describes the yearly flooding of the Nile.

Irrigation is a way of supplying water to dry land through a system of channels.

Julius Caesar was a general who became the Roman emperor.

Mark Antony was the Roman general who married Cleopatra.

Mummification is the process of preserving a body before burial in ancient Egypt.

A **nilometer** is an instrument used to measure the rise and fall of the Nile.

A **nomarch** was in charge of the administration of a region, or nome.

Papyrus is a type of paper made with reeds. Ancient Egyptians wrote on papyrus.

A **pharaoh** was the ruler or king of ancient Egypt.

Pyramids were tombs and were thought to protect the souls of pharaohs.

Resin is a waterproof substance secreted by many plants.

The **Rosetta Stone** was discovered in 1799 by a group of Napoleon's soldiers.

Senet is an ancient Egyptian board game similar to backgammon.

The **vizier** was the chief adviser to the pharaoh.

Lab pages

Photocopy these sheets and use them to make your own notes.

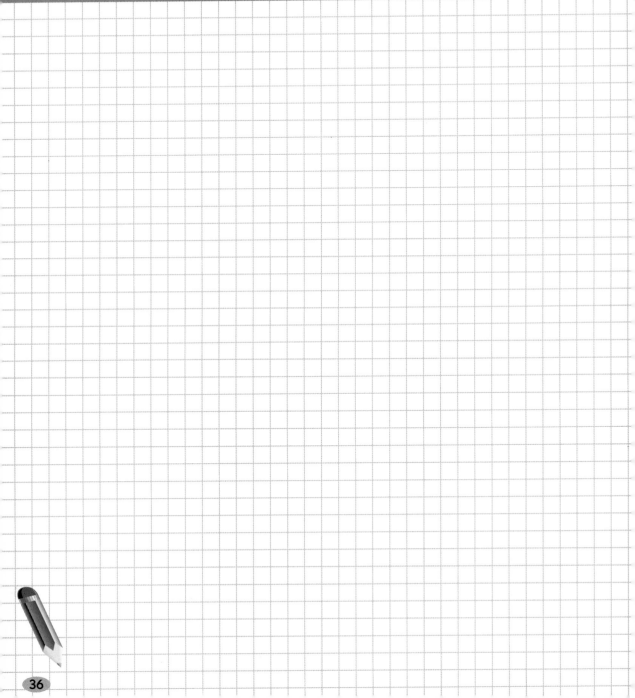

Rules of senet

Senet was one of the ancient Egyptians' favorite board games. It is a two-player game – so you'll need someone to play against. Choose an opponent. The rules are easy to learn.

▲ **All the counters move in a zizag path across the board.**

▲ **The board is divided into 30 squares, and each player has seven counters. To start the game, take turns throwing the four sticks into the air until one player throws a one. You score a one when one stick lands face up. This player gets the blue counters, and the other player gets the red counters.**

Once you have scored a one to start the game, you must then score a two or a three to move each piece from its starting position. If none of the throwing sticks lands face up, the score is five.

You cannot move a piece into a square that is already occupied by one of your own pieces.

You can move a piece into a square that is occupied by one of your opponent's pieces. If you do so, you must trade places with your opponent's piece.

You cannot trade places with one of your opponent's pieces if it is next to another one of your opponent's pieces.

You cannot jump over a row of three or more enemy counters.

You can decide how you want to split up the value of your throw among your pieces. For example, if you throw a three, you can move three pieces one square each, or one piece two squares and another piece one square.

On the board there are five squares with special marks on them:

▲ House of Water.
If you land on this square, you must move back to the House of Rebirth square.

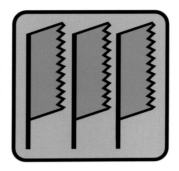

▲ House of Rebirth.
A counter must return to this square if it lands on the House of Water square.

▲ House of Joy.
All counters must land on this square before they leave the board.

▲ House of Amon-Re.
If a counter lands on this square, it is stuck there until a two is thrown.

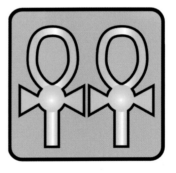

▲ House of Three Truths.
If a counter lands on this square, it is stuck there until a three is thrown.

If one of your pieces has been sent back from the House of Water square to the House of Rebirth square, and there is already a counter there, you must move your counter to the first free square behind it.

You must move if you can, and you must use up the whole value of your throw, or forfeit your turn.

The winner is the first player to get all his or her counters off the board.

Loading your INTERFACT disk

INTERFACT is easy to load. But, before you begin, quickly run through the checklist on the opposite page to ensure that your computer is ready to run the program.

Your INTERFACT CD-ROM will run on both PCs with Windows and on Apple Macs. To make sure that your computer meets the system requirements, check the list below.

SYSTEM REQUIREMENTS

PC
- 486DX2/66 Mhz Processor
- Windows 3.1, 3.11, 95, 98 (or later)
- 8 Mb RAM (16 Mb recommended for Windows 95 and 24 Mb recommended for Windows 98)
- VGA colour monitor
- SoundBlaster-compatible soundcard

APPLE MACINTOSH
- 68020 processor
- system 7.0 (or later)
- 16 Mb of RAM

LOADING INSTRUCTIONS

You can run INTERFACT from the disk – you don't need to install it on your hard drive.

PC WITH WINDOWS 95 OR 98

The program should start automatically when you put the disk in the CD drive. If it does not, follow these instructions.

1. Put the disk in the CD drive
2. Open MY COMPUTER
3. Double-click on the CD drive icon
4. Double-click on the icon called EGYPT

PC WITH WINDOWS 3.1 OR 3.11

1. Put the disk in the CD drive
2. Select RUN from the FILE menu in the PROGRAM MANAGER
3. Type D:\EGYPT (Where D is the letter of your CD drive)
4. Press the RETURN key

APPLE MACINTOSH

1. Put the disk in the CD drive
2. Double click on the INTERFACT icon
3. Double click on the icon called EGYPT

CHECKLIST

- Firstly, make sure that your computer and monitor meet the system requirements as set out on page 40.

- Ensure that your computer, monitor and CD-ROM drive are all switched on and working normally.

- It is important that you do not have any other applications, such as wordprocessors, running. Before starting INTERFACT quit all other applications.

- Make sure that any screen savers have been switched off.

- If you are running INTERFACT on a PC with Windows 3.1 or 3.11, make sure that you type in the correct instructions when loading the disk, using a colon (:) not a semi-colon (;) and a back slash (\) not a forward slash (/). Also, do not use any other punctuation or put any spaces between letters.

How to use INTERFACT

INTERFACT is easy to use.
First find out how to load the program
(see page 40), then read these simple
instructions and dive in!

You will find that there are lots of different features to explore.
Choose the feature you want to play using the controls on the right-hand side of the screen. You will see that the main area of the screen changes as you click on different features.

For example, this is what your screen will look like when you explore Smart Art – an Egyptian wall painting that you can examine on screen. Once you've selected a feature, click on the main screen to start playing.

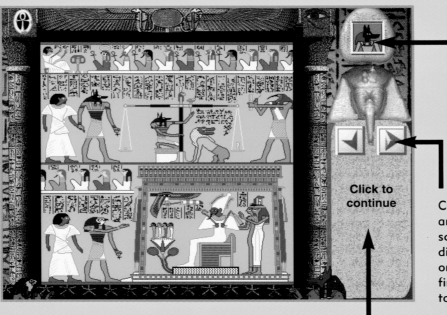

Click here to select the feature you want to play.

Click to continue

Click on the arrow keys to scroll through the different features on the disk or find your way to the exit.

This is the text box, where instructions and directions appear. See page 4 to find out what's on the disk.

DISK LINKS

When you read the book, you'll come across Disk Links. These show you where to find activities on the disk that relate to the page you are reading. Use the arrow keys to find the icon on screen that matches the one in the Disk Link.

DISK LINK
Learn how to make an Egyptian mummy by exploring I Want My Mummy on the disk.

BOOKMARKS

As you explore the features on the disk, you'll bump into Bookmarks. These show you where to look in the book for more information about the topic on screen. Just turn to the page of the book shown in the Bookmark.

23

LAB PAGES

On pages 36–37, you'll find grid pages to photocopy. These are for making notes and recording the results of any of the book's experiments you carry out.

HOT DISK TIPS

- After you have chosen the feature you want to play, remember to move the cursor from the icon to the main screen before clicking the mouse again.

- If you don't know how to use one of the on-screen controls, simply touch it with your cursor. An explanation will pop up in the text box!

- Keep a close eye on the cursor. When it changes from an arrow ➔ to a hand, ☞ click your mouse and something will happen.

- Any words that appear on screen in blue and underlined are "hot." This means you can touch them with the cursor for more information.

- Explore the screen! There are secret hot spots and hidden surprises to find.

Troubleshooting

If you come across a problem loading or running the INTERFACT disk, you should find the solution here. If you still cannot solve your problem, call the helpline at 1-609-921-6700

QUICK FIXES Run through these general checkpoints before consulting COMMON PROBLEMS (see opposite page).

QUICK FIXES

PC WITH WINDOWS 3.1 OR 3.11

1 Check that you have the minimum system requirements: 386/33Mhz, VGA color monitor, 4Mb of RAM.

2 Make sure you have typed in the correct instructions: a colon (:) not a semi-colon (;) and a back slash (\) not a forward slash (/). Also, do not put any spaces between letters or punctuation.

3 It is important that you do not have any other programs running. Before you start **INTERFACT**, hold down the Control key and press Escape. If you find that other programs are open, click on them with the mouse, then click the End Task key.

QUICK FIXES

PC WITH WINDOWS 95

1 Make sure you have typed in the correct instructions: a colon (:) not a semi-colon (;) and a back slash(\) not a forward slash (/). Also, do not put any spaces between letters or punctuation.

2 It is important that you do not have any other programs running. Before you start **INTERFACT**, look at the task bar. If you find that other programs are open, click with the right mouse button and select Close from the pop-up menu.

MACINTOSH

1 Make sure that you have the minimum system requirements: 68020 processor, 640x480 color display, system 7.0 (or a later version), and 4Mb of RAM.

2 It is important that you do not have any other programs running. Before you start **INTERFACT**, click on the application menu in the top right-hand corner. Select each of the open applications and select Quit from the File menu.

COMMON PROBLEMS

 Symptom: Cannot load disk.
Problem: There is not enough space available on your hard disk.
Solution: Make more space available by deleting old applications and files you don't use until 6Mb of free space is available.

 Symptom: Disk will not run.
Problem: There is not enough memory available.
Solution: *Either* quit other open applications (see Quick Fixes) *or* increase your machine's RAM by adjusting the Virtual Memory.

 Symptom: Graphics do not load or are poor quality.
Problem: *Either* there is not enough memory available *or* you have the wrong display setting.
Solution: *Either* quit other applications (see Quick Fixes) *or* make sure that your monitor control is set to 640x480x256 or VGA.

 Symptom: There is no sound (PCs only).
Problem: Your sound card is not Soundblaster compatible.
Solution: Try to configure your sound settings to make them Soundblaster compatible (refer to your sound card manual for more details).

 Symptom: Your machine freezes.
Problem: There is not enough memory available.
Solution: *Either* quit other applications (see Quick Fixes) *or* increase your machine's RAM by adjusting the Virtual Memory.

Symptom: Text does not fit neatly into boxes and "hot" copy does not bring up extra information.
Problem: Standard fonts on your computer have been moved or deleted.
Solution: Reinstall standard fonts. The PC version requires Arial; the Macintosh version requires Helvetica. See your computer manual for further information.

Index

A

afterlife 16
Akhenaton 13
Amon 14, 15
Amon-Re 13, 15
Anubis 14, 16
astronomy 9, 10

B

Bast 14
Bookmarks 3, 43

C

CD-ROM 40
children 20, 25, 28
Cleopatra 13
clothes 28
craft 24
crops 10, 26

D

desert 10
Disk Links 3, 43

E

education 20

F

farming 10, 27, 24, 27, 34
floppy disks 40–41
food 22, 26, 27
furniture 22, 23, 24

G

games 25
gods 12, 13, 14, 15, 16
government 9, 12, 13

H

Hathor 15

Help Screen   4
hieroglyphs   20, 21, 34
house   22, 23, 24

I

Inundation   10, 27
Isis   15
I Want My Mummy   5

J

jackal   15
Journey of Discovery 5

L

Land of the Pharaohs   4
loading instructions for your disk
   40–41

M

Menes   9
mummy   17

N

Nile   8, 10, 11, 26, 34

P

papyrus   20

pharaoh   8, 9, 12, 13, 18, 26
pyramid   8, 18, 19, 24

R

Riddle of the Sphinx   4

S

scribes   20, 21, 24
senet   5, 25
Smart Art   4
sphinx   9
system requirements   40, 44–45

T

tax   12, 27
temple   8, 14, 15, 22
Thoth   16
tomb   8, 14, 20, 22, 34
transportation   11
troubleshooting   44–45
Tutankhamen   13
Thutmose III   13

W

Write Away   5